D1357053

If you understand how the mind of a dog works in relation to its moods, reactions, impulses, instincts and association of ideas, you are indeed lucky. Then all that is needed to own a happy well-behaved companion is that the owner should use common sense, coupled with training, in its character forming; not the services of a dog psychiatrist to achieve this relationship.

Barbara Woodhouse proves this point beyond a doubt in her book.

KNOW YOUR DOG

Know Your Dog

Psychiatry or Sense?

BARBARA WOODHOUSE

BARBARA WOODHOUSE
CAMPIONS, CROXLEY GREEN,
RICKMANSWORTH, HERTS

Reproduced and printed in Great Britain by
Straker Brothers Ltd.
Whitstable

CONTENTS

ILLUSTRATIONS

Foreword

Many people will think it funny to write a book about dog psychiatry when I don't think this possible or practical. A lot of rubbish has been talked about the psycho-analysing of dogs in the modern world, and I feel, having now trained over 13,000 dogs in ten years, I am qualified to express an opinion on the subject.

For years I have been receiving data for this book in letters from desperate or depressed owners whose dogs are causing them worry or despair. I feel I must help them further by de-bunking many ideas about dogs and their minds. Then at least their lives may be made more normal and their owners happy.

If dog owners recognise their dog's failure and their own personal problems, this is a hopeful sign. For many people realise only too well that even though they have owned perfect dogs in the past, today's vintage may not be the same. Their old theories and methods may be completely out of date.

With vast experience behind me I believe that unless a dog is unapproachably savage or mentally unsound, it can be made a decent member of society and a joy to own. Thus was coined my school motto, which is: 'There is no such thing as a difficult dog, only an inexperienced owner.'

I sincerely hope this book will open the eyes of many to their dogs' natures, help those in trouble and give hope to the despairing. Many will criticize what I say, but I have spared no one, least of all myself.

I

The Mind of the Dog

'Psychiatry' is defined in the dictionary as 'the study of mental disease'; 'psycho-analysis' as 'the treatment of nervous ailments in which the causes are traced to forgotten concepts in the mind'. This quickly damns psycho-analysis as being applicable to dogs, and the pyschiatrist as assuming that all naughty or difficult dogs are so because of mental disease. If this is the case I reckon at least a million of our dogs alive today should be hastily destroyed, as psycho-analysis is impossible with dogs since they cannot answer questions. Therefore the concepts of the mind cannot be recalled and probed and changed, cast out or anything else.

That does not mean that anyone cannot understand the working of the dog's mind or thoughts, whichever you wish to call it, for telepathy on the part of dog and owner plays a vast part in the happy companionship between dog and mankind. Hundreds of times in my life I have shown in public that I know exactly what a dog is thinking at a certain moment, but I utterly refuse to believe anyone knows what it was thinking in the past, and this is essential to the skill and work of a psychiatrist.

People are gullible. Invent a big word, charge fees and, with the help of a working knowledge of dogs, one can get away with murder. A human personality can be so powerful that it can make the dog do and think things almost by hypnotism, just as a good actress can carry the audience to the height of happiness or despair with the part she is playing. But, when the curtain drops, the atmosphere fades and the audience returns to its mundane thoughts. That is why I have refused and shall continue to refuse to take dogs to train without their owners. I know I can make a dog do almost exactly what I wish when alone with it. Without the disturbing mental reactions of the owner, the dog is mine in will and thought.

But will a dog that carries out orders with army-like precision for me, with evident joy on its face, do the same for an owner who may be out of tune with the dog, either from lack of experience or sympathy, or from just being plain stupid, conceited or pig-headed? I know it won't. Then the partnership is doomed from the start. The dog becomes unsure of itself, the owner becomes unsure of the dog and the trainer becomes unsure of both. He is sure only of the necessity for the owner to train himself or herself as much as the dog.

I have heard a thousand times a year the complaint, 'I have had dogs all my life but this one is so different,' often with the added remark, 'You are my last hope. If you can't train him, I shall put him to sleep.' That very remark appalls me when the poor dog is often only a puppy and maybe his crime consists of tearing up furniture, or biting the children or adults in the house, or barking or whining incessantly. The owners have completely failed to find out what is the most likely cause of the trouble. They tear off to the vet, who may have little experience in the training of dogs, for his job is their health. Often the advice given by the vet is not what a trainer would give. Tranquillisers, for instance, only mask the real fault and, in the end, the owner realises that the dog must either be trained or put to sleep. Tranquillisers can only be a temporary measure to give the owner rest, or confidence, or both. For the dog they mean a dulling of its mind and body, but more about these later.

What governs the behaviour of a dog? How far does its mind think? What can be put down to instinct? I think that, before the puppy is 8 weeks old, instinct is nearly 99% of the dog's mind, and the control of its actions is almost entirely guided by the desire to eat, sleep, keep warm and play. After that the human contacts it makes, the discipline it receives, and the affection it develops for the person who nurtures it, begin to play an important part in the forming of the dog's mind and character.

No two people are alike, no two dogs are alike. We often see in the same litter an entirely different make-up in character and looks. Although it helps to study pedigrees and see the parents of the dog you are going to take into your home, it is no guarantee that the dog will be anything like the last dog you had with similar breeding, or even like the rest of the litter he was born into. This is where owners trip up badly. They feel 'done in the eye' if the breed that was previously a joy to them lets them down. They assume, for example, that all Border Collies are easily trained, affectionate and nice to own. They get extremely annoyed if their small puppy bites them, or won't come when called, and maybe is dirty in the house, when their previous one made none of these mistakes. From that moment the dog hasn't quite the same loving owner as he had when he was purchased and he subconciously picks up the irritation of his owner by telepathy. He becomes aggressive because the owner is not feeling too well disposed towards him, and a vicious circle is started in more senses than one.

To train a dog with sympathy and understanding one must try to understand a dog's mind. That mind has several big thoughts, its body a few major requirements. Firstly, the body governs the mind to a great extent when the puppy is young. The need to eat, sleep, urinate and defecate are the main factors. It hasn't entered a dog's mind that it is wrong to puddle on the floor or soil its bed. Its reactions are entirely spontaneous. When scolded for these things it does not at first connect its action with the cross words and 'fear' enters its mind. Nature's reactions to fear are many: some animals crouch and stay as still as if dead; others snarl and attack the thing or person that frightens them; others turn on their tummy believing this age-old action of a baby animal will help them; some urinate and open their bowels with seemingly no control whatsoever. Most young animals rush to drink from their mothers if frightened.

In training dogs we must take all these things into consideration before we punish a dog and look upon it with disappointment or disgust. Only by repetition do dogs know what is right or wrong when very tiny. Their minds cannot reason what is right or wrong. They learn from experience of the tone of voice of the owner, or the resulting jerk on a choke chain, or by being put into their kennels when naughty or any other punishment that the owner has thought to be suitable. But, whatever the punishment, it is not always effective, for one has to gauge the natural reaction of the dog's mind to the treatment it is receiving or is about to receive. In many instances this reaction is to bite the person that is reproving it, or to lick and jump up on the person who is praising it. That is why, in my school, I am very loathe to correct a keen and loving dog from jumping up in the early stages of training, for, if you repress its natural exuberance and show of affection in the only way the dog knows, you may also be inhibiting the dog's natural love for you.

I think this love is of paramount importance and I constantly hug, kiss and play joyfully with my pupils even if I have had to be extremely firm with them to achieve initial obedience. The result is that there enters the dog's mind a memory of affection and fun rather than fear of correction. For, make no mistake, dogs don't object to fair correction. In fact, if you face up to it, the most loving dogs often seem to belong to owners to whom I would hate to be related in any way. A dog longs for love and it thinks that by fawning on a horrid owner it may achieve its desire, and so keeps on fawning *ad infinitum*. But woe betide the owner who refuses to face up to the fact that a dog's mind is not a human mind, and firmly believes that any correction given to the dog will be remembered by that dog for ever and held against the owner.

The dog has an enviable mind; it remembers the nice things in life and quickly blots out the nasty. That is why, when people tell me their small puppy was attacked by a big dog and that in later life made him into a fighter, I say, 'Bunkum!' If your dog wasn't a fighter by nature, he wouldn't be one. Forget the past and deal with the present. Face up to the fact that his hormone balance or his hereditary characteristics are far more likely to make him into a fighter than having been attacked by another dog. After all, in the wild state, dogs were always attacking each other, and even play amongst dogs consists of biting and knocking each other over. Lack of firmness and leadership by the owner is far more likely to cause emotional upsets in the dog than a previous attack by another dog.

2

Love, Honour and Obey

In the dog's mind, a master or a mistress to love, honour and obey is an absolute necessity. The love is dormant in the dog until brought into full bloom by an understanding owner. Thousands of dogs appear to love their owners, they welcome them home with enthusiastic wagging of the tail and jumping up, they follow them about their houses happily and, to the normal person seeing the dog, the affection is true and deep. But to the experienced dog trainer this outward show is not enough. The true test of real love is when the dog has got the opportunity to go out on its own as soon as a door is left open by mistake, and it goes off and often doesn't return for hours. That dog only loves its home comforts and the attention it gets from its family; it doesn't truly love the master or mistress as they fondly think. True love in dogs only comes when every door can be open and the dog will still stay happily within earshot of its owner. For the owner must be the be-all-and-end-all of a dog's life.

To achieve this the owner has to master the dog at some time or other as the leader of the pack did in bygone days. There must be no question as to who is the boss of the house; it must be the owner. Dogs not only love owners who have had at one time a battle of wills for supremacy, they adore them, for a dog is really a subservient creature by nature, longing to trust his true love to someone's heart.

Now we come to the word 'honour', or, as I prefer it, 'respect.' This respect in a dog's mind is paramount, and I can't repeat often enough that, without respect which includes a certain amount of 'righteous fear' as the Bible would say, the dog lacks something in his essential make-up which sentimentality cannot replace.

When I use the words 'righteous fear' women in particular shrink with horror; they wouldn't like their dogs to be frightened of them. When I explain that righteous fear is not being frightened, they don't understand. The reason humans don't all steal, lie or what have you, is simply because in most of us there is a righteous fear of the results. In dogs it should be the same. If they run off or fight another dog, their minds must be educated to know that there will be a reprisal and, without this righteous fear, the dog will never be completely happy, for dogs love looking up to their owners or, as the case may be, their trainers.

It is indeed very sad for me to see the number of dogs whose minds are forever tuned-in to mine in a class when they should be tuned-in to their owners' thoughts and wishes. The reason is, I make them immediately do as I wish and then give abundant praise. Many owners, in a distorted sense of kindness, let the dogs get away with disobedience, or make them do it so slowly that there is no respect for the owner from the dog. In fact many dogs show this in no mean way by biting their owners. When a dog bites its owner I feel sure it is mostly done as a last desperate resort to rouse the owner into being someone the dog can respect. Once the owner has got that respect the

dog can be taught everything with the least possible number of scoldings or corrections. A dog loves to learn things
and adores to please. Once the hurdle of respect has been
jumped, the continuation of training goes smoothly.

This sequence of events is very hard to teach the owners,
for a vast number of dog owners have no idea what their
dog prefers. They think dogs adore sentimentality. Dogs do
up to a certain point, but even the tiniest of toy dogs wants
a proper owner to love and respect; just because he only
weighs 2 lbs that doesn't mean he has no character or that
he should not be obedient. People are now finding out that
the tiniest Yorkshire terrier, for example, has a brain big
enough to do first class obedience; its mind works the same
as a Great Dane's mind; it also wants to respect its owner.
There is no difference between men owners and women
owners as regards over-sentimentality. In fact I have found
some men to be more stupidly sentimental than women
and when I have to be firm with their dogs they feel very
badly about it. Yet the dogs show which they prefer and
every time it is the strong-minded but loving handler who
gets real love and implicit obedience from the dog.

If a dog is cringing and frightened I always know the
owner has not been firm enough with it, for this type of
dog needs someone to respect more than any other; it is
weak-natured itself and likes to draw courage and strength
from a firm owner.

What do I mean by the word 'firm'? I use it so often that
people may think I mean, 'Get a stick and beat the dog.'
This is far from my mind. In fact I think owners should
practically never smack a dog, for it is a sign of defeat on
the owner's part. It means that the dog's progressive train-

ing and the development of its mind and intelligence has
not been accomplished. It means the owner has to resort to
something that may be beyond his own strength. It is de-
grading for both dog and owner, for a dog that has been
firmly but kindly trained never needs a beating. No, firmness in my estimation means a firmness of purpose, a
strength of will that doesn't take defeat however long it
takes to succeed. A firmness that is gentle as well as strong,
for, make no mistake, a disobedient and wilful dog needs
prolonged patience and perseverance to win.

By being firm I mean setting the dog something to do
and making him do it, knowing in your own mind that
that which you wish him to do is fair and right and necessary for his and your happy co-existence. He may fight,
scream as if being murdered, or just bite you in retaliation,
or may just seem mortally afraid; all these ruses can be
tried on by a dog when asked to obey. If you are not firm
your inner heart revolts at making him obey and you are
sorry for his whimperings or his apparent fear or defiance.
You let up and let him get his own way. The seeds of dis-
respect are sown and will accordingly germinate, to the
ultimate misery of both owner and dog.

Often in my class I meet these disrespectful dogs who
don't truly love their owners. But the owners are mightily
annoyed when I tell them their dogs don't really love
them. They assure me the dog never leaves them in the
house, etc; but it cuts no ice with me. I know that once I
have shown the owners how much their dogs prefer me
to them after I have made them carry out my wishes they
will be converted. I think the old motto, 'You have to be
cruel to be kind,' should be changed for dog owners to,

'You have to be firm to be kind.' Firmness only has to be continued until the right kind of respect enters the dog's mind. And, when being firm, unending praise and affection must be given to the dog.

This praise and affection is where a multitude of owners fail their dogs. A pat and a kind word are not enough in the initial training of dogs; the atmosphere must be charged with a certain excitement, for dogs are very sensitive to excitement; when they have done right, they love having the wildest show of affection and a good romp round. Dull owners make dull dogs, stony-faced owners, zip-lipped owners, and inhibited owners tend to have dull disobedient dogs, who take a long time to learn obedience.

The dog's mind is only equal to a child's mind and, as comedy makes up a big part of a child's life, it should do the same in a dog's life. Dogs love laughter, clapping and jokes. I had a little dog who laughed when we laughed although she hadn't the slightest idea what she was laughing about. It was the happiness that pervaded the room when we were laughing that entered her brain and made her feel happy so she smiled too. Try smiling at everyone you meet down the street; you will be amazed how many complete strangers smile back before they zip up again realising they don't know you. It is the same with dogs even if they don't know you; they respond to a smile and a clap if they have done well. They watch your eyes and face for the happy sign that you are pleased. I am intensely sorry for the dogs who see no smiles on their owners' faces. You can't train a dog well if you are unhappy; your tenseness communicates itself to the dog, and the dog becomes depressed.

What a wonderful indicator of happiness is the dog's tail; the half-mast wag with the very tip of the tail, showing nervous expectation; the half-mast slow wag of the interested dog who wants to know what master is saying but doesn't quite pick it up; the full-mast wag of excitement and happiness when he is really happy; and, last but not least, the tail between the legs of the nervous, shy or unhappy dog who trusts no one and to whom life is a burden.

When a dog is happily learning, or happily obeying I like to see its tail at the medium sensible height; when having a game after lessons or when free I like the full mast. But what I like most is to change in a matter of minutes the tail between the legs to the half mast by firm and sensible handling, for this can be done in minutes if you get through to the dog's mind and give strength to it by your own forceful happiness and strength of purpose. A dog that loves, honours and consequently obeys is a joy to himself and his owner.

3

Sex

Everyone who has a lot to do with the training of dogs can't help but notice that bitches are far easier to train than dogs. The reason is that, except when she is 'on heat' or in the throes of a 'pseudo pregnancy,' a bitch's attention is not disturbed by matters of sex – although greyhounds are not raced within three months after being on heat, because they are supposed not to be at their best at those times. A bitch is better tempered than a male dog on the whole, for the fighting instinct for supremacy over other dogs is not so prevalent, although bitches do get extremely jealous, especially of their own offspring. I have known mother and daughter fight incessantly so that one has to be parted with. This often happens in the human race – mother and daughter don't get on – so it is nothing new to us to find it in the animal kingdom as well. Sex is a thing no so-called psychiatrist can fathom, for the dog again cannot answer questions as to whether his sex life is normal, or whether he had unpleasant sexual adventures when young. Therefore the dog owner must rely on experience of sexual behaviour in dogs and use that knowledge to make the dog's existence healthy and happy.

Many dogs literally seem to have minds that rely almost entirely on sex for most of their lives, and these oversexed dogs are a curse to themselves and their owners; they are abnormal and should not, in my opinion, perpetuate the race, for in these days of built-up areas and lack of free run for dogs an oversexed dog is a curse. You can't get through to their minds at all without intensive training for long periods and with a greater degree of firmness than, in my opinion, is kind. I say with all my heart that, unless the owner of this dog particularly requires it for show purposes, it should be 'doctored' to make its life happy and that of its owners equally trouble-free. Wild cries of, 'I shouldn't like to do that to my dog,' or, 'I would hate to take its nature away,' are bound to be heard from ignorant people who don't know enough about castration, whose vets have little or no personal experience of it or from people who know someone who knows someone who had their dog done and it got fat and dull. What they didn't bother to find out was, what was the owner of the castrated dog like? Did that owner feed the dog every time it asked for food? Did they reduce the food that they had been giving it, as it was no longer using up energy fussing over sex matters? Did they give it reasonable exercise and sufficient training to make its life interesting? These are the factors that make a castrated dog no different to any other dog except that it is happier in every way and a joy to own in town or country, with or without other dogs. Only when sex is a nuisance need this be done, and I heartily recommend it to everyone, whatever the age of the oversexed dog.

What goes on in the mind of the oversexed male dog? The answer is, nothing but the desire to copulate. It doesn't really matter whether the bitch it meets is on heat, it often doesn't matter whether the dog it meets is male or female, it is quite happy to carry out its sexual exercises on the leg of a child or even the furniture. It growls ferociously at other dogs, willing to fight any of them due to nervous sexual excitement; it often bites its owner in a fit of frustration. It barks or whines most of the day and cannot at any time be made to attend with proper concentration when there are other dogs about, whatever their sex. Many people think they will cure this oversexed menace by letting him 'have a bitch'. How sorry they will be if they do this! All the full flood of sexual fulfilment makes the dog after that a maniac, for now his instincts are more fully aroused than ever and discipline becomes more impossible than ever. Yet get this dog alone in some place where no dog has been, and no smells or dogs are about, and he will often be the nicest possible dog, gay, loving and obedient.

Why then are owners so queer about castrating dogs? I have had over 400 dogs done on my advice, and in every case the owner and dog are happy where formerly the dog was impossible, the owner fed-up, and the partnership in grave danger of being ended. But these owners are taking my advice as to diet of a strict nature and are continuing the training of the dog, for castration takes time to work until all the hormones already manufactured in the dog's body are exhausted; but even after 3 weeks most owners note a difference. The normal male dog shows no interest in a bitch not on heat, and only cursory interest in a bitch on heat for her first week; he shows no interest in mounting other male dogs, furniture or people's legs and will leave smells and lamp posts alone when trained in obedience. He is seldom a fighter.

There have been dogs that are unstable because they are hermaphrodite, i.e. they have two sexes in one body. This causes dogs to be bad-tempered and unreliable, as are the male dogs known as monorchids or cryptorchids. This means they have only one or neither of their two testicles descended into the scrotum. Castration in these cases is difficult and a major operation. In normal cases it is a simple and uneventful operation done by an experienced vet; no stitches need be inserted and the dog can return home in under 24 hours.

The dog's mind is not adversely affected by castration. There must be no ideas in the owner's mind about denying the dog its natural pleasures; an ordinary dog doesn't get these 'natural pleasures' unless it is a stud dog or belongs to a bad owner who allows it to wander and have promiscuous relations with any bitch it meets. Dogs who have no desires don't fret because they have lost these desires; they love their owners more dearly; they are gay, happy dogs, not deluded miseries cursed by too many hormones.

After all, sex in a dog cannot be looked upon in the same way as sex in humans. Dogs don't have sex hormones for any other reason than to perpetuate the race and, with this object in mind, will get thin and miserable when a bitch is on heat in the neighbourhood; will travel miles, making their feet sore, in spite of hunger and thirst, to wait hopelessly outside a bitch's home; will take even a beating without noticing it in the attempt to attack or carry out sex impulses with other male dogs; and will destroy floors or furniture and fittings in sexual frustration. The mind of a dog doesn't look into the future if its sex organs are to be removed; it doesn't anticipate a loss of pleasure; it has a general anaesthetic so knows nothing about the operation. Three or four days later nobody would know the dog had had anything done to it except that it remains the same gay dog it always was and becomes more interested in the odd snack between meals!

With bitches this oversexed characteristic doesn't exist; the spaying of bitches, except in case of disease, is not to be recommended from my experience. It is a dangerous operation; the bitch does become duller, and there is a tendency to get fat. This does not mean that I think every bitch should breed a litter for her health. I think that utterly wrong. It has been proved in veterinary circles that bitches bred with are more susceptible to uterine disease than those not bred with. Many over-sentimental people worry when their pets, obviously keen to get with a dog, fret a bit and, although puppies are not wanted, they mate the bitch 'for her own sake, bless her.' I think they are wrong. There are too many unwanted dogs in this country today to warrant breeding for this reason.

Only bitches and dogs with some special points should be bred with and never if temperament is bad. Breeding will not make a bad-tempered or shy bitch or dog better tempered or non-shy; all that is being done is passing on to unfortunate dog owners a bad-tempered dog. This particularly applies to owners of Alsatians whose temperament is deteriorating in so many cases.

If a dog is mentally unhappy with its sex and shows it by fussing at all times about other dogs, castrate it. You are being kind, not cruel, to the dog and all who meet it.

No psychiatrist can help the dog by mind reading. Sex is above all that nonsense. Firm training can do a lot, but take an experienced trainer's advice. No dog-loving trainer will tell you your dog is oversexed if it only lacks training.

4

Praise

The mind of a dog is forever open to take in, by touch, by telepathy, and by talking, the feelings, ideas, emotions and wishes of its owner. That is, if the dog loves its owner. To get through to a dog's mind you don't need a couch and sweet music or probing questions from a psychiatrist. You need hands that on touching the dog send messages of love and sympathy to its brain. You need a voice with a wide range of tones to convey aurally your wishes and feelings towards the dog. You need eyes that tell the dog who watches them what you are feeling towards it, even though it may be hidden from the outside world, and above all you need telepathy so that the dog thinks with you.

These things are not always born in people. They can be developed as any sense or gift can be developed. That is, providing the person who wishes to develop them is honest in mind, because with animals you cannot cheat; it is useless watching a trainer handling your dog with hatred of her in your heart, or dislike of all the things she is doing which you think unnecessary or harsh, or both. If you give an order to your dog by word of mouth and are feeling sorry for it inside you are doomed to failure. Dogs above all creatures love honesty of purpose. If you pat a dog and your fingers are not carrying that loving message you don't deceive the dog.

No one knows why touch is so important. I think probably blind people know more than any of us about the sensitivity of touch; that is why guide dogs are usually so faithful. But the ordinary handler can develop this touch which calms the wild dog, which produces ecstasy in dogs when you caress them, but it has to come through the fingers or face direct from your heart. In every training school the words 'Praise your dog' are heard constantly; by those words in my school I don't necessarily mean a big hearty pat. I mean a communion of brain and touch. I lay my face alongside that of the dog with its face cupped in my hands, and I sense that my deep love and admiration for it passes right through to its mind, often in silent communion, for I have already said 'Good dog' and clapped my hands to show approval at the end of the exercise. But a dog needs more than that if you are to get its complete mind in tune with yours. Unhappy are the handlers who think this all stuff and nonsense. For it makes dogs truly happy.

Lots of dogs have to put up with second-best praise but, if you can't let yourself go, you must at least mean what you say when praising. The tone of voice must convey great joy to the dog. It must convey to him that you think him the most wonderful dog on earth, and you must never mind what other people in the school are thinking. Half the trouble in training schools is the natural restraint and reserve that stifles people in public. They cannot forget themselves and abandon themselves to working and praising or correcting the dog.

In the same way, it is difficult for most of us to correct our dog in the street for fear of what people will do or say or think. If we truly loved our dog other people and their thoughts wouldn't matter, but it is easier to write this than to carry it out. The general public are so ill-informed on the training of dogs that I am certain the R.S.P.C.A. get a multitude of phone calls from oversentimental ignoramuses who haven't the foggiest idea what goes on in a dog's mind, and who think it cruel to correct a dog firmly. They mix up discipline with cruelty, and would apparently rather see a dog run over or put to sleep than have it corrected in the street when it has done wrong. But the handler's life is almost in danger by correcting a dog in public in the effort to make it eligible for the praise to follow.

It is extraordinary how dogs pick up praise straight from your brain almost before you have had time to put it into words. A dog's mind is so quick in picking up your thoughts that, as you think them, they enter the dog's mind simultaneously. I have great difficulty in this matter in giving the owners commands in class for the dog obeys my thoughts before my mouth has had time to give the owner the command. I find it extremely difficult to correct a dog for this, although it shouldn't really be obeying me; it should be tuned into the owner who of course doesn't know what I am going to say until I have said it – that is unless the owner is also telepathic.

In the same way I know what the dog is thinking as it thinks it, and can often therefore stop it being naughty or disobedient before it has erred, which saves correcting it and helps quick training. But I find the chattering that goes on in class by those people who don't truly concentrate very hampering to this mind communication. It is like

having constant interference on a wireless set. But then I
don't suppose many people know what a thrill it is to be
on the same wavelength as a dog.

Praise can be given in so many ways, by titbits for a
puppy, by tone of voice, by scratching a dog's chest, by
firm warm pats on the back, by kissing, which all dogs
love, or by just looking straight into their eyes and smiling.
You can't deceive dogs. It doesn't matter whether you say
'Good dog' or 'Gadzooks'. The dog knows what you mean.

5

Correction

The correcting of a dog inevitably gives more pain to the owner than it does to the dog; the resulting effect on the mind is far worse for the owner than for the dog. Dogs are the most wonderful creatures to own because they don't brood over the past, they don't hold a grudge against their owners, they seem to know when correction is fair and just, and they definitely have consciences, which to me proves they also have souls, although I am told this is not possible and in the next world we shall not see our dogs again!

This book is not to help those dogs for whom a pained look is enough to make them crawl in shame, nor those who listen for the sad tone of voice which denotes the owner's displeasure. Rather it is for those dogs whom the owners erroneously thought psychiatry could help. The dogs we are dealing with are problems in some way and the more gentle and persuasive treatment is unlikely to work on them.

What can a handler do and what is the effect on a dog's mind? First of all I believe most correction can be done with a jerk on the choke chain providing the choke chain is the thick-linked variety, not the watch-chain type which is cruel. This sharp jerk has a wonderful effect on the dog; it does not pain him but it shocks his mind into thinking, and a shock, however caused, is much more likely to be remembered than a scolding. Everyone knows in medical practice these days shock treatment by electric impulses is given to nervously unstable patients. I believe the same sort of thing happens to nervously unstable dogs when jerked hard on a choke chain. I have cured the most cringing, terrified dogs in a matter of minutes, not days, with a few sharp jerks, the cupping of my hands round their faces and a lot of cheerful encouragement.

One boxer got a First at Crufts with the report, 'What a wonderful temperament'; had the judge seen this dog three days previously she would have had to lie on the floor to inspect it. The owner was terrified when she saw me jerk her kennel rope, but was soon won over when she saw the almost instantaneous response. I have seen nervous Alsatians, terrified of everyone and dirty in the house because they were too nervous outside to perform their duties, become sound in mind and consequently immediately clean in the house when cured of nerves by this method.

After much thought I have decided that the effect of correction on a dog's mind is to give it confidence, a happy respect for its handler and a longing to be with the person who carries out the correction. No one quite knows why some dogs are excessively nervous. Even with faultless pedigrees showing no hereditary nerves or viciousness you get these pathetic creatures that many people despair of and put to sleep, when really there is absolutely no need for this if they can be cured in hours. They obviously have inner horrors such as fearing to jump into a car; they are terrified of going upstairs, horrified at the sight of a man or a child, neither of whom have ever done the dog harm. I get hun-

dreds of letters from people who assume this fear is due to
possible ill-treatment in the past, but this is most unlikely;
few people really ill-treat a puppy. I know it to be mostly
nervous instability, cause unknown.

Most people who have these nervous dogs coax them,
sympathise with them, don't go in cars if the dog doesn't
wish to accompany them, don't make the dog go upstairs
if it is frightened, don't make it talk to men or children if
frightened, and generally put up with a lot of unhappy in-
convenience to, as they think, help the dog. This has a
disasterous effect on the dog's mind, for he picks up the
sad sympathy of the owner's mind, senses the gentle pull
on the lead when he won't walk on it, and the nervous
tension of the owner struggling to help him. The terror
gets worse and worse, and the owner usually, on vet's or
incompetent trainer's advice, puts the unhappy dog to sleep
when it has often had under twelve months of life.

My heart bleeds for these misguided owners and their
dogs. If only they knew how easy it is to change these nervous dogs, they would be happier. But first they must
understand a dog's mind. They must harden their hearts
and realise that what they are going to do to the dog is for
its good, in the same way as a surgeon cuts off a limb to
save a life; he doesn't squirm at the ghastly business of
chopping off the limb, he looks forward to the regaining
of health and life in the patient. I treat dogs in the same
way. I know if I can shut my ears to the occasional terrified
squeaks of the terrified dog and continue without emotion
to jerk it on, that in about 10 to 15 minutes, I shall have
won. The dog will stop being frightened, the cure will
have begun. It is then only a matter of teaching a dog

routine exercises to strengthen its sense of security.

But my greatest handicap is to get the owner in the right frame of mind. Some of them need shutting in somewhere away from the dog whilst the cure is going on; they should only be released when the dog is cured. But if you did this they would not see for themselves how the cure was carried out; they would not pick up the confident way the dog progressed, and above all, they would not see the loving way the dog responds to the correct handling. Definitely this cure must be with the co-operation of owner and absolute trust in the trainer, for sometimes it is necessary to muzzle a very nervous dog since otherwise, in their initial fear, they attempt to bite. This must never be allowed. The handler must be completely safe in carrying out this correction, for the slightest fear on the part of the handler will undo all the good the jerking has done.

Many dogs object at first to a muzzle and they struggle to get it off. The sentimental owner wrings her hands in suppressed sympathy. The atmosphere is charged with emotion, although really there is nothing cruel about a muzzle. Greyhounds wear them all the time when out. Dogs in Italy and other foreign countries wear them for protection against rabies. Many dogs with bad temperaments in this country would be far happier free with muzzles than kept snarling on a short lead. For, whilst the dog is muzzled, the owner need not fear a fight, for a dog can do no harm in a well-fitting muzzle. I have muzzles far too large for the dog so that drinking and panting is in no way stopped. After a few minutes the dog doesn't worry about a muzzle and usually under a hour later it can be discarded. Only for the initial safety of handler and dog is it occasionally necessary to use one.

The next type of correction is a good shake. The dog needs grasping by his choke chain and scruff on both sides of his neck under his ears, and whilst looking the dog straight in the eyes scold in a thunderous tone and give three or four hard shakes. This will calm an hysterical dog and will make a 'don't care' one listen to you. It is a correction that makes the dog feel slightly silly, and he doesn't want it repeated, I have seldom had to shake a dog more than twice. It needs strength with a big dog, but it is of course a dog's own answer to unruliness in the pack. Dogs shake each other in play or fight and, when the handler does it, she is only being a better dog than the dog itself, which is an attitude all dogs respect.

Shutting a dog up and not speaking to it as a correction is quite stupid. The dog's mind doesn't understand this sort of correction at all. You can punish humans by sending them to Coventry; you can only lose a dog's deep affection by the same treatment. A dog's mind can't reason that, because he ate the Sunday joint, he is being shut in the outhouse or not being spoken to. His simple mind either frets for your companionship or goes off to find something interesting to amuse him and ends up by tearing up the floor or some other evil.

The dog's mind is not to be compared with even a child's mind. His conscience only acts when he knows from long contact with his owner that he has done wrong, by her attitude of mind he senses that he has done wrong, but unless correction is given at the moment of the wrong action, he won't remember what he has done. That is why smacking a dog when he comes back to you having run off for hours is useless. To him you are smacking him for coming to you – he doesn't remember he ran off hours ago. That is why in my school I personally try and catch dogs running away from their owners and give them a whack with the end of a soft leather lead on their backsides. It is being caught in the action that teaches a dog. I hate any owner to smack a dog. Let me be the horrid person that has to do it if all calling fails.

What a dog's mind can interpret is being put as a punishment into the 'down' position and being made to stay there until he feels more disposed to co-operate with his handler. This has a wonderful effect on hysterical dogs, barking dogs, fighting dogs and obstreperous dogs, and I strongly recommend anyone with a naughty dog to master the act of putting her dog into the down for short spells at a time. The dog is under control in the down and his mind recognises your mastery over him. Dogs like being mastered – it gives them a nice safe feeling and of course makes them respect the handler.

Lastly, smacking a dog as a punishment is only to be used as a last resort and should be used if a dog without rhyme or reason attacks another dog or person. The inflicting of pain on him at these attacks is an 'eye for an eye' and is a quick and effective deterrent for a very serious crime. But the smacking should if possible be done with a leather lead over the dog's rump. Never hit a dog with a newspaper or on its face. No crime should ever involve a newspaper; it is ineffective and really annoys and hurts the dog's mind.

No dogs are permanently hurt in mind or body after three or four whacks with a leather lead, but I have known it cure a fighter caught in the act of aggression. The whacking of a dog inevitably hurts the handler more than the dog, and those in poor health cannot do it. In my school no pupil is ever allowed to smack a dog. If it has to be done I do it myself – without temper and sufficiently hard to make the dog feel it without harming it at all. All dog lovers hate doing it or watching it done, but in some cases dogs are so stubborn as to have no finer feelings, and this is the only effective treatment. It may save them from being put to sleep.

In all cases of correcting a dog the handler's character has to be taken into consideration, for most dogs' faults are really handlers' faults and the faults in handlers' temperaments are multitudinous. I think hundreds of them should never own a dog but, as there is no law that permits dogs to be taken away from stupid owners, the poor dog has to be made to conform to the owner whatever the state of mind or the condition of the owner and his home surrounding. I am often terribly, terribly sorry for dogs that come to me. I long to keep them and give them a sensible existence, but all I can do is to make misfits fit as far as is within my power. At the end of many of my training sessions I almost need a psychiatrist myself!

6

Jealousy

In the case of jealousy the mind of a dog works in almost an identical way to that of a human being. It wants the full attention and love of its owner whether jealousy only occurs when another dog enters the home or when the beloved owner talks to another dog outside or whether it be aimed towards another person in the home, the same driving force is at the root of the evil – the intention of the dog to reign alone and supreme in that household.

The guarding instinct so prevalent in some breeds has its roots in the same sort of thing – a desire to let no one enter the precincts of his master or mistress. Jealousy nearly always takes the form of a show of viciousness towards the dog or person the animal is jealous of. Quite often it is a mild form of jealousy and only involves its bone, toy or the piece of rug that it is fond of. It jealously guards them and woe betide anyone trying to take that object away.

This jealousy is particularly pronounced when puppies are reared and kept in the household. As the puppy reaches the age of about three months the mother will begin to feel jealous as her maternal instinct fades and the time draws near for another 'on heat' period. In spite of trying to treat both dogs equally and always talking to both at the same time, feeding both at the same time and exercising both together, the jealousy continues to grow.

Correction works at first and then bit by bit grows less effective. In the dog's mind a usurper has entered and, as in the wild state the young are turned out of the nest and abandoned, the dam is trying to do the same thing in the home. As she fails to get rid of the now grown-up pup her temper gets worse and worse in the effort to dislodge the now adult and unwanted member of the household. She becomes more and more thwarted as her owner attempts to make the newcomer as welcome at the old-established member, and often she turns on her owner when that person is trying to make peace, as if she were trying to impress an ignorant person that it was time the youngster went out into the world to fend for itself.

If you are a really good handler your training methods will be good enough to make both dogs obey the command 'leave' when they are in your presence. The danger lies in the times you leave the dogs together on their own, for the slightest boldness on the part of the youngster in approaching the older one's basket or toy, etc, infuriates the older dog and she sets on the youngster tooth and nail. Sometimes the mother is a killer and, unless kept apart from her offspring, would no doubt have a go at killing it. Such is the age-old instinct to get rid of the young before it is time to breed again. Luckily this instinct is not very common. Generations of domesticity have dimmed it considerably, but I have met it, mostly in smaller dogs, and I am sorry to say that I have not been able to give much hope to the owner of curing it.

Most dogs show a streak of jealousy at some time or other When my own two dogs used to come to my bedroom, if I talked to the Dane the little English Toy terrier would jump on the bed and have a go at nipping the Dane's nose in spite of the fact she was smiling all the time so that her own face would receive the pats and kisses the big one was getting, and she would also have got, but there was a streak of jealousy in her nature which did not appear in the Dane's. But then I think little dogs possess this factor in a more marked degree than big dogs, who are more placid.

Jealousy occurs when two terriers are hunting. If one catches a rat the other will often try and take it away, not because it wants it – most good ratters instantly leave their dead quarry to find other live ones – but simply because the dog is jealous, and wants to be equal with the killer.

Biting of husbands or wives is a very common form of jealousy. The dog senses that he is not the be-all-and-end-all of a beloved owner when the master of the house comes home, and therefore if the husband gets near his wife, he may get bitten. The answer to this one is for the husband to master the dog in no mean way by leaving a string on its choke chain and, when it attempts to be nasty, giving it an almighty jerk and a scolding, then petting and loving it. Then the dog will recognise he is the boss and all dogs are happy to submit to a real master.

Few men dare do this with their wives' dogs for fear of upsetting their wife or, in some cases, literally being attacked by their wives in defence of the dog, for some wives would rather have their husbands bitten than allow the husbands to correct the dog. How silly can some women be, for surely the life of the family depends on the happiness of all concerned and the dog is as much part of the family as a child. I encourage husbands to watch their wives training their dogs and sometimes to take over the training. It forms a happy camaraderie in the attempt to make the dog a 'joy to all and a nuisance to no one'.

In the curing of this husband-biting complex the wife must try and feel really annoyed if the dog attacks for, make no mistake, a dog picks up the thoughts of the wife without a word being spoken and, if it thinks the wife doesn't really disapprove of having her husband bitten, then the dog will continue to do so. But if she feels really angry about it and so does the husband, the combined waves of disapproval floating about for the dog's mind to pick up will be strong enough for the most insensitive dog.

Correction by the mistress of the dog in these cases seems to fail, the reason being that the dog doesn't respect the person it is jealous of. Otherwise it would live in a peaceful co-existence. The person of whom the dog is jealous must do the correcting and often this is an old grandmother or grandfather whose physical strength does not permit them to handle the dog in the right way. Then there is little hope of a cure and the dog must simply be kept out of the way of the person it is jealous of. It must not be the other way round, asking the person to keep out of the way. A human being must always come first in these matters or the dog will realise it is supreme and become worse and worse as its ego gets stronger support.

Dogs are seldom jealous of small children. The mind of a dog looks upon small children as it would look upon its own whelps. That is why even fierce dogs are seldom known to hurt children. The Alsatian that killed a child was obviously frightened by the tripping of the child who may even have caught its ear or something in falling. The

1. Telepathic communication

2. All breeds of dogs can be trained by common sense

3. Dogs trained on a weekend course by the author

4. Chica smiling

immediate reaction to fear in a dog is to bite or kill your enemy and that dog in my view was temporarily deranged with fear. I do not believe it was a naturally savage dog.

A nervous dog is always a potentially dangerous dog. That is why I always curse the breeders who sell these creatures and who breed litters from problem dogs, hoping their traits won't come out in their offspring. This hope is not often fulfilled. Nervous parents teach their puppies fear by telepathy from an early age, and, if the bitch feels fear, the puppies automatically follow suit. Only with training, from an early age if possible, will the fear be eradicated.

Jealousy in kennelled dogs is particularly rife in stud dogs. Each stud dog wants to reign supreme over the kennel wives and, when there are a number of stud dogs there, it is wise to keep them apart. Although dogs are polygamous by nature, they often choose a favourite wife. I clearly remember my Alsatian choosing a wife and going off with her to our orchard and digging a 15 foot underground passage and bedroom at the end for her to have her litter in; his other wives were just for business purposes only, this one was the true mate. She was allowed by us to have her 9 puppies down there and to see Argus standing erect on top of the entrance the day she whelped was a thrilling sight, for we felt the true nature of the dogs had been allowed to develop by choosing their own home, and bringing up the babies in a homely atmosphere.

Only when the babies were 14 days old and near to weaning time did we interfere. They were the most wonderful litter we had ever bred. But I have never seen or met with instinct like that before or since. When we opened up the nest it was beautifully made round a corner of the passage with straw and hay the bitch had picked up in her mouth, plus masses of her own hair she had plucked from her chest. The nest was scrupulously clean and dry; in fact she was a model many human mothers could have copied.

I don't believe there is any cure for jealousy in stud dogs. I think, if some of them had the chance, they would fight to the finish and that is too near nature for the dog trainer to be able to do an efficient job, although I do recommend muzzling and exercising them together if the breed is not too big. Naturally if dogs are properly obedience-trained from the start these things seldom occur, but the average breeder has no time or wish to carry out obedience training for fear it may spoil the character of the show dogs. Most of us trainers know that, far from doing this, it enhances a dog's chance of winning by its perfect ring manners. I still hope the day will come when no working breed gets its championship title without also having obtained some simple obedience title.

A trained dog's mind is educated; the look on its face is quite different from the scatty brutes one often sees in the ring. It has an aura of warm friendly confidence sadly lacking in many show dogs. By having supreme confidence in its handler it rests quietly at a show if she has to be parted from it, and that counts for a lot when you require a dog on the peak of its form even after a tiring day. The mind of a dog can absorb so much that it is child's play for it to carry out obedience exercises when wanted and yet still remember to stand and be examined and to walk and run as required for the beauty ring. It only means that a few different commands are learnt, and that is no difficulty to an intelligent dog. If it is not intelligent it shouldn't win prizes, for who wants a stupid dog with no mind of its own?

Now that we are on the subject of jealousy I think some of my pupils are a bit jealous themselves when I work their dogs, and should realise that only by years of experience have I learnt anything about the training of dogs; they cannot expect to work a dog without learning the art the hard way, that is hard work, patience and the willingness to learn something new every day from someone. None of us know it all, and the pupil who rushes in here with a know-all attitude will not learn as quickly as those who watch and listen, eager to assimilate knowledge.

Every dog is different and, although they all undergo identical training, it is only by reading their minds and watching their reactions that progress is made. Most human pupils are wonderful the way they patiently try to follow suit in the training methods and I think some of their dogs are absolutely beastly to be unco-operative to such loving owners, but a dog's nature is governed by a multitude of instincts and reactions and none of us really knows it all.

I have tried castration for jealousy amongst male dogs not wanted for show or stud and it doesn't work. This is the one vice it doesn't touch, which proves that jealousy is a mental thing not a sexual one. If the dogs are both sent to boarding kennels or a trainer they will show no signs of jealousy and will live peacefully together again until such a time as they adopt that place as home, then the trouble starts all over again. All of which goes to prove it is true jealousy as suffered by the human race, not lack of training or an hereditary fault.

7

Fighting

Fighting dogs are the ones that give most worry to owners. It is this vice which owners hope a psychiatrist will be able to probe and cure but once again I stress that, since this is the process of investigating into the past of a dog's mind which cannot be probed as the dog cannot answer questions, one can't progress. That does not mean we cannot understand a dog's present state of mind. Although past events may have had disastrous effects on the dog and have affected his mind and make-up, it will have to be the owner who is psycho-analysed to find the answer to the dog's problems. But as few owners would have the nerve or sense to go to a human doctor to find out why her dog fights, I think we can leave out this subject too.

A dog fights for several reasons, usually the right to survive, whether this be taken as the right to eat and live peaceably or simply that the dog wants to live up to a certain standard whereby he has no enemies or neighbours that irritate him. We do not know which fits each individual case. What we do know is that dogs pretend to fight in play, mauling each other in a rough and tumble which nobody minds. Puppies have mock fights all the time to strengthen their limbs and develop their jaws and to wear off their superabundance of energy, but the subject we are looking at here is serious dog fighting, which is

FIGHTING 45

dangerous for dogs and humans, and has been known to end in death for the smaller and weaker dog. Even if the fight is not so bad as to end in death it can cause the owner of the dog to have a heart attack from fear, it can cause people to be bitten, and is most unpleasant and terrifying to say the least of it.

Most people don't realise it takes quite a minute for two dogs to get really to grips, and that before that they are playing for a hold, and therefore, when you go to separate a dog fight, there is no need to rush in and get bitten. It is far safer to watch at close range until you can safely get a hold of collar, or loose skin between the eyes of the dog. Once it has got a hold on the other dog it is unlikely to turn round and bite the person trying to release its hold, so you are reasonably safe when it has got a hold in slipping a lead on, or grabbing the choke chain or scruff.

It is useless beating the dog; they are mentally unaware of pain at that moment and unless you knocked the dog out you would not hurt them enough to separate them once they had a real hold. A mild dog fight, where death is not the object of the aggressor can sometimes be stopped by beating when the dog has no collar, but the best method if two people are about is for each on the word 'now' to grab their collars and hold them off their front legs so they begin to choke; it takes terrific strength to do this with big dogs, so I grab the flesh on the forehead between the eyes and they let go at once with this. Moreover they cannot bite you.

What is in the dog's mind when it attacks every dog it meets or just has one enemy round the corner? Most of it is a show of strength, very often a cowardly show of

strength aimed at other people's toy dogs who can't answer
the bully back. Face that same bully with a big dog likely
to answer back and it will disappear into the distance, for
the dog knows who will be boss even in its own race and,
if it senses superiority of physique or brain, it will automatically be subservient. That is why young dogs lie on
their backs, all four feet in the air, when they meet an older
or stronger dog; they know who is boss and are showing
the other dog so by giving the 'pax' sign which is exposing
the tummy to an enemy. That is why I tell pupils that this
trick is not a nice one really and should be checked at an
early age, for it is purely one of a weak animal giving in to
a stronger one in mind and usually an enemy at that. Few
owners would like to think their dogs look upon them as
enemies, but that is the case. When a dog no longer looks
upon you as a potential enemy it stops this lying on its
back as protection, though many dogs in later life do it because their owners have scratched their chests which they
like, and they hope for it again. But primarily it belongs to
the defence mechanism of the dog tribe.

The mind of a dog that fights always has at the back of
it the wish to be the boss of the tribe, and he fights other
male dogs who are sexually mature to make sure there is
no risk of his being questioned as 'lord of all he surveys'.
Muzzle that dog and let him loose with the dog he has
previously fought and nine times out of ten he will realise
he is at a disadvantage and show no signs of aggression.
That is why I muzzle fighters and free them with trained
dogs or non-fighters. They then learn to enjoy themselves
in a community and the wish to fight goes. Often, having
muzzled, introduced and trained them for a short time to-

gether, I have formerly bad fighters lying side by side without muzzles after a few minutes.

Your own personality needs to be strong to deal with fighters, because fighters are usually adult dogs. Few puppies fight, few bitches fight, therefore your mind must be stronger than that of the potential fighter so that you are the boss, not either of the dogs. If the dog is sex-mad you can do nothing but castrate it. Muzzling is only a palliative not a cure. Those who won't have the operation performed on their dog should always muzzle these dogs in public places. There is nothing so terrifying as having one's dog attacked when out on peaceful business with a well-trained dog. I had my dog attacked in the post office when put to the sit and she did not answer back the boxer who attacked her. I really suffered from shock after it as I think anyone would seeing their own much beloved dog attacked, coupled with the physical effort needed to drag a fully adult male boxer off one's dog. Had my dog been a fighter I do not believe I should have had the strength to keep them apart when separated, and few people will help one in these emergencies.

I think owners of fighting dogs should be prosecuted if their dogs are ever allowed free in public places unmuzzled. I know of several cases where innocent poodles have had severe injuries and one of a dear little fox-terrier bitch who had her leg broken by boxers in a London park. That little bitch will never be well. The boxers live to do it again; their owners are quite irresponsible.

Many dogs that fight are undoubtedly mentally unsound, just as mad as mental human beings in lunatic asylums. But there are no lunatic asylums for dogs, only trainers who must know, if they are honest, that many of these dogs are incurable and all the training or sentiment in the world won't help them. If firm training and/or castration doesn't stop them I think they should be put to sleep, muzzled when out or never brought into contact with other people's dogs. I have met few really mad dogs and, with the right instruction and veterinary treatment, I have only advised that ten of my dog pupils be put to sleep out of 13,000.

Jealousy, sex, and the guarding instinct are the three things that cause most fights; the dog's mind only runs on those lines unless he is a starved dog and fights for food, unlikely in this year of grace for dogs belonging to readers of this book. The cure is firm handling and training, castration in really bad cases, and the treatment of the dog by freeing it with other non-fighting dogs under supervision.

The breeders of these fighting dogs should be heavily punished as quite a bit of it is hereditary. No fighter should win a prize in any show.

One can usually read the mind of the dog about to fight seconds before it attacks, by the stiffening of the legs and the raising of the hair along the back and the sort of springy walk as if the dog was on hot bricks, and the slightly curved walk forward which means the dog is ready to turn instantly should his foe attack his quarters. If you are tuned into your dog's mind you will pick up by telepathy the previous tenseness before any of the visible signs appear. If you are exercising a fighter you should always be on the *qui vive*. A thunderous command 'Leave' often brings a dog to its senses and no fight occurs.

8

Food

To what extent does food govern a dog's mind? This is a question that most owners have had to face up to at one time or another, and many of them have told me they think food occupies most of the waking and thinking hours of their dogs. But I am quite sure that the people who own such dogs are very unlucky.

The hunting instinct is extremely strong in most dogs; therefore, with problem dogs that chase and kill chickens or other livestock, the act is only what nature taught them to do many thousands of years ago. Their noses were designed for the act of tracking down and killing and, although domesticity has vastly reduced the number of breeds who hunt to kill, greyhounds, foxhounds and like breeds still in fact have this instinct highly developed. Many other breeds would hardly know what to do with the prey they had killed as they no longer suffer from hunger and, without this urge to spur them on, the kill is not vital.

In the wild state dogs killed twice or three times a week and ate until they nearly burst, after which they were quite happy to laze between orgies. Nowadays from an early age our dogs' gastric juices have been trained to flow at fixed times each day and the desire to eat only becomes apparent normally at these times. It is true there are greedy dogs who will eat at all times of the day and night to the detriment of their figures and health, but these are the dogs that are easily trained by bribes.

The dogs that are the most difficult to bribe are the naughtiest ones, because their minds are usually fixed on fighting another dog or running off into the distance, and I doubt if they think food will come from these escapades. The dogs who are most interested in food are the spoilt poodles and toy dogs whose adoring owners give them snacks at all times. 'Just a leetle bitsie for Mitzie' has been known to do devasting things for Mitzie's mind and body, but here I blame the owner more than the dog.

Undoubtedly stealing food in a young dog is a training fault as well as a veterinary fault, for many dog thieves commit this crime because they have worms and are always hungry. The food is not doing them as much good as it would be minus these parasites. The actual act of stealing is of course a training fault and has to be treated as such. The teaching of food refusal in obedience tests was a very useful lesson to most dogs as people in shops often offer one's dog a titbit; when the dog turned his head away and refused to take it, it taught the shop-keeper not to repeat the offer. But it also had a disastrous effect on dogs sent to boarding kennels, as many refused to take food from the strange person who fed them and in one known case the dog nearly died. So now this test has been omitted from the schedule.

It is quite certain that the mind of the dog controls its expectation of food, and one hardly needs a timepiece in the house because a dog's saliva will commence running at exactly the same time each day in expectation of a feed,

and it is always best to feed at regular hours if you wish
your dog to stop pestering you at all hours. The same thing
applies to food as an aid to training. If a puppy knows it is
going to get a titbit if it comes when called, or retrieves
a dumb-bell, it is naturally going to do that thing if feeling
hungry, but it also means that, if you stop giving it titbits
it reasons you are a fraud and is then more difficult to
train than ever. I therefore maintain that titbits should not
be used except in exceptional cases when all other methods
have failed.

This is especially important in the case of castrated dogs
whose diet has to be rigidly controlled, old dogs whose
figures have already exceeded normal girth, and greedy
dogs who would never be satisfied with the small amounts
given to them and would therefore get more cunning in
the hope of getting more food. Nervous dogs wouldn't take
the food or, if they did take it, would probably be sick
almost immediately because the nerves have an adverse
effect on digestion; and to feed a dog suffering from nervous exhaustion does more harm than good. That is why I
never allow the dogs to be fed during a day's training. I
always tell the owners to wait an hour after training ceases
and then give the dog one big meal and let it rest.

I am sure the most important thing about food in connection with the dog is to give a properly balanced diet
with sufficient vitamins and iron, etc; for a dog to be intelligent it has to be sufficiently and adequately nourished.
If a dog is lacking minerals it will eat rubbish and especially
dung. How can one expect to train a dog to be a nice companion in the house if it forever rolls in nasty things, eats
manure and has a depraved appetite? Again no mind-

reader can fathom the depths of a dog's mind and find the answer to its apparently depraved nature. Only common sense and knowledge of the dietetic needs of a dog learnt from experience, books or your vet will help you.

Everyone knows that human beings either smoke or eat when worried and often an unstable dog will steal when it is upset or frightened. That is why dogs often steal when they are left alone in the house when they wouldn't dream of doing so when the owner is at home. The dog lacks security and eating helps this feeling for some unknown reason; the only answer I can think of is that more calories are used up when a dog is worrying than when it is content.

9

Indulgences

This is a chapter that needs much thought both from the point of view of the dog and that of the owner, I think more in the case of the latter. For is there one of us who at sometime or other in our lives cannot plead guilty to having indulged our dog? The mind of the dog tunes in very willingly to enjoy as many indulgences as it can persuade its owner to offer. Its brain is never slow to take advantake of every kink in the defence armour of its owner. The eyes of a dog, the expression of a dog, the warmly wagging tail of a dog and gloriously cold damp nose of a dog were in my opinion all God-given for one purpose only, to make complete fools of us human beings.

I write reams about over-sentimental dog owners spoiling their dogs, yet know in my inner heart that not to do so takes supreme will power. For dogs are champions at heart-stealing. Even the wickedest dog in my school who has severely bitten me makes me long to hug him close to me and force out his evil wickedness, and I love him. Dogs are not slow-witted. They know when to push the slightest advantage they gain over their owner. How many dogs do we know who have committed some sin and who have cleverly evaded punishment by bringing mistress something to play with and, with an innocent look of deep trust, waited for her to join in the game when at that very moment she should be stick in hand flaying the life out of him? But then that is the fascination of dogs.

Why do hundreds of us give up our holidays to stay with them, cry our eyes out when we lose them, defend them against all those horrid people who don't love them and on our death beds make provision for them in preference to our needy families? It is because there is something about a dog that gets you. Even if you own a problem one with all the evil the devil himself invented, you still know that, inside that dog, there is something very lovable – a dog that will never criticise you, a dog that doesn't care whether you are from the top or bottom drawer, who doesn't care whether you are clever or stupid, beautiful or hideous, rich or poor. He is yours and you are his.

That is why a chapter on indulgences is difficult to write. For I in my own mind know that we can all read the dog's mind when he looks at the best chair, looks back to owner and again back to the chair, that it clearly means, "May I get up?' It takes a stony heart to refuse, though we know we should.

At my residential training school of the past I am sure I have shocked pupils by feeding my dogs at meals. They don't ask. They just lie down waiting hopefully. My contention is, if my dogs don't annoy me and if I want to feed them, who is to say it is wrong? That is how I look upon all indulgences. If you like your dogs to sleep on your bed, putting up with the discomfort of not being able to turn over easily (especially if yours is a Great Dane) having a snoring bed companion, risking the hairs and dirt on the blankets and sheets, well, that is your business. What is *my*

business, as a trainer, is to see these things don't happen
if you wish otherwise.

This is where a dog needs firm training, for a multitude
of dogs get on their owner's beds and refuse to get off
without a struggle and often bite the owner in the process.
This is where a psychiatrist would easily be able to help,
for he would know that, in the past, the dog had got away
with it and it needs no probing of the mind to know the
dog much prefers a lovely warm bed with a warm owner
in it, possibly a hot bottle, and certainly an eiderdown, to
his own meagre offering of a basket and a blanket.

There is no doubt at all in his mind that dogs love
luxury. 'Liver' instead of 'lights', beds instead of baskets,
kisses instead of kicks and, if the owner doesn't want to
bestow any of these luxuries on the dog, then the struggle
to deny them to the dog must begin the moment the dog
enters the house and must be carried on to its dying day.

My own dog, star of thirty-seven films, winner of sixty-
seven obedience prizes, herself defeated rigid obedience at
the ripe old age of ten and a half years. Never in her life
had she been allowed to lie in front of the fire. The heat is
not good for dogs. She was too big and took up too much
room. Her digestion was not so good that Camay was her
only scent. Nevertheless when we moved house she felt
she would like a change and with audacious abandon lay
full length in front of the fire.

At first we laughed. Then I said her name in a shocked
voice. She smiled a sickly smile and the tip of her tail
wagged, uncertainty backed by hope and then, sensing my
sympathy for her aging self, downed her head and feigned
sleep. I pulled myself together and one word, 'Sofa!', was

enough to have her leap to her feet and climb on her own extremely comfortable sofa. You see her mind had picked up by telepathy that I didn't really mind her in front of the fire. In fact I thought she looked rather beautiful with her brindled body outstretched. My own mind was weak. The dog knew at once. You cannot train a dog if you are weak or oversentimental. They know and you are lost.

Are indulgences wrong for dogs? I think, under certain circumstances, no. What does count is, can you give up indulging the dog without fights or disagreeable behaviour the very moment you wish? If you can't, don't indulge your dog until you have trained it sufficiently well to be able to do what you wish at any time. The day the dog takes over you are lost. I do think one indulgence is very wrong, that is when you cannot leave your dog alone without its screaming or barking; should anything vital happen so that you could not stay with it, the neighbours would have to suffer appalling noise and you and the dog would be utterly miserable.

I think dogs should always go with their owners whenever and wherever possible. Yet some places you go to don't admit dogs. Occasionally you are ill and may have to go to hospital or to a clinic. The dog can't go with you; it must stay at home or in your car. If neither of these things have been taught by previous training and endless tests, you won't know what to do. This sort of situation is bad. All dogs should be taught to stay quietly at home for some hours; as long as their routine is not broken too violently and they have been fed and exercised, there should be no hardship in staying at home for a dog.

We know titbits are bad for dogs; we know sleeping in owners' beds is inclined to overheat them and make them delicate; we know above all that giving a command and then not having it carried out is fatal to a happy relationship. We know over-indulgent owners get spoilt dogs a joy to none and a nuisance to all. I suggest we have a happy medium. Let's spoil our dogs sometimes, then we shall all be happy. The happiest people in this world are those that are for ever giving and making others happy. I am sure our dogs are included in that.

10

Rigid Obedience

This chapter may shock fanatic obedience fans. I have been one of them more by force of circumstances than desire. When Juno, my Great Dane, was six months old I decided to take her up to the final test in obedience exercises and win in that class at shows – not because I am a lover of rigid show obedience but because, if one is to be a trainer of other people's dogs, one must be capable and experienced in matters relating to training. I had already trained dogs for Police work, Guard work, and film work and as companions; now I would do obedience tests as laid down by the Kennel Club. I wanted to find out what were the reactions of a much-beloved highly intelligent dog to the set schedule.

These are my findings: Dogs will do anything in the world for the owners they love. They will retrieve ridiculous articles like candles in spite of their horrid flavour. They will attempt to pick up spanners, fir cones and anything else deemed suitable if the owner wishes it, even though their mouths were not designed to hold that type of article. They will tolerate chairs dropped behind them, strange people trying to force them to eat food their owner doesn't wish them to eat. They will lie down on freezing concrete or too hot asphalt just because the owner wills it. They will ignore other dogs for minutes on end, not even scratching themselves, for fear of losing a mark for the owner it seems to mean so much to. They put up with having their ears pulled by fans after winning 1st prize, in the vain hope that soon they will be able to go home and be dogs, not automatons any more. They will suffer the torture of not having a beloved owner look at them or smile at them in the course of an exercise, and of being almost sent to Coventry with only single words of command to break the silence. This and a lot more a dog will put up with. They will learn the exercises just for the owner. They will rejoice with the owner when the exercises are over, hoping that each one is the last, and when the owner is tired of showing off in public what a wonderful power he has got over his dog, the dog will willingly return to being a nice jolly companion doing crooked sits and sniffing interesting scents.

The best working dogs are in my opinion highly strung, nervous dogs; the worst, placid ones who do obedience but wouldn't win prizes. To say dogs are happy doing competitive obedience, in unnatural conditions, for no possible reason, except as a self-booster for the owner, is self-deception. To carry on obedience until the dog is too old to move fast enough to obey, is downright cruelty. No one loves an obedient dog more than I do. For short spells I believe dogs like doing faultless sits if the owner is thrilled about it, and smiles and praises with obvious enthusiasm. But what dog can possibly enjoy the tensed-up owner who strides martially round the ring, hand strapped over the chest, lips zipped, expression nil? No! dogs don't like obedience carried out like that. To have freedom to carry out a difficult exercise with skill, encouragement and the combination of two minds as one, would be a joyous sight and occupation for dog and owner.

I retired Juno from the obedience ring at 11 months – 5 months too many as far as she was concerned. She and I knew it all; in fact we knew so much that I shall never work a dog again in the obedience ring. I will train dogs for it if their owners wish, for I may be wrong, but, as for inflicting these conditions again on one of my own dogs, I definitely won't.

How can the mind of a dog always be ready to receive so much concentrated obedience without tiring? The conditions of the ring where these gyrations are carried out are often appalling to a sensitive dog. Some dog may have puddled where our dog is to lie down and stay down for fifteen minutes. Does any self-respecting dog like to lie down where normally he would go round that spot? Does he find it difficult to hear audible commands when the public watching are making such a noise? Yet one distraction and a little bit of inattention and the dog has lost marks. The owner is furious inside, even if to please the public he pats the dog as if it didn't matter.

I have yet to meet the person to whom it doesn't matter, if they are really honest. Can all this be happy for the dog? Can his mind really comprehend why straight sits, nose on owner's leg, etc, is so important? I think not. In fact I think long spells of obedience the most tiring thing for a dog; there seems no logical end to it. For dogs a red prize card isn't a quarry hunted down or a successful track and a criminal apprehended. In fact, except to please the dog's owner, any obedience that needs barrack square performance must seem futile to an intelligent dog.

I believe all dogs should be trained in essential exercises. These are: Heel on and off the lead; Come when called; Sit and stay there; Down and stay there; Drop on recall instantly; Leave other dogs, livestock and things alone. This training should be commenced not later than three months old and should be ended as soon as the dog is competent. The owner should at all times convey to the dog by praise, speech, and smile that he has done well. By tone of voice, jerks on the choke chain or an occasional slap, if absolutely necessary, that he is a bad dog.

By the time these essential exercises can be carried out efficiently and happily on the part of the dog, kindly owners know they have done their duty to the dog and mankind. What more they do is done solely for business purposes or for the owner's pleasure and ego. I doubt if the dog is considered.

11

Guarding

How does the mind of a dog work in this matter of protecting the household it belongs to and their property? I believe under the age of twelve months old it hardly reasons it out at all. People who ring me up and tell me their five-months-old puppy is useless for guarding their house need to understand that, if a puppy barked and guarded at that age, in all probability it would be savage and a pest when adult. The development of the mind in different breeds of dogs varies vastly. A St Bernard might not be fully developed at two years old, whilst a terrier may behave like a grown dog at twelve months. One cannot compare breeds or individual dogs development as regards their protective instinct, or their desire to be a guard dog.

The upbringing of a dog counts for so much in these matters. Most puppies of up to say six months or over are boisterous and friendly to all, unless they have nervous temperaments, and that is how it should be. If they are put out into the garden for long periods to find their own amusement they will probably become scatty, and bark at everyone for a long time. The reason for this is that the early developing mind of a dog doesn't know who or what to guard. But when kept in the house with its owner the place to be guarded is quite plainly defined in the dog's brain. The garden however is a very different matter, especially in a built up area with lots of people passing by.

At first the dog is quite good, he only barks at people who enter the premises, then he finds to his delight that they pause when he barks, and he begins to feel superior and important; thus his lack of respect towards mankind commences. Next he tries barking at people walking down the road, and passing dogs, cars, bicycles, etc; perhaps even starts running up and down the fence with his hackles up, showing all and sundry what a brave dog he is.

He gets bolder and, as a tradesman enters the gate carrying something, he goes up to him barking. The tradesman automatically raises in the air whatever he is carrying to get it out of the way of the dog, and the dog interprets that as a sign of weakness, his ego grows, his fierceness increases and now people who enter the gate find quite a nasty dog barking at them, who refuses to go to the owner who is calling him or to stop barking when told. They back out of the gate and shut it in his face. That act alone annoys the dog and the result is, he bites the next tradesman who comes in. That is how a nasty-tempered dog takes his first bite at a human being.

In the dog's mind he is not only keeping strangers away from his home, but he is showing his superiority over man. Unless he can be quickly broken of this habit he will get worse. The owner is powerless to make him stop barking because he has probably not been trained to come when called, and therefore he wins all round.

If however a dog is systematically trained to give warning of the approach of everyone to the house by barking when kept in the house, the owner can easily make him stop doing so by making him lie down with the command 'cease' followed by 'down'. If he doesn't stop a sharp jerk on the choke chain will do the trick. The dog recognises authority, and quickly learns that to bark in the first place receives praise, but not to stop barking when told earns him a reprimand.

If he is so stupid as to not understand, the only cure is a prolonged session in the 'down' position for about 10 minutes. There is nothing so subduing to the excitable dog as this and most indiscriminate barking is due to excitement. That is why, when the telephone goes or the doorbell rings, dogs become hysterical.

Many people are proud of the way a young puppy guards and boast about it to their friends, but they will be more than likely sorry if they don't check it when the puppy is still young. I think twelve/fourteen months plenty early enough for a puppy to show signs of aggression towards strangers, and even in this case on the command 'cease' and a further command 'talk' the dog should cease barking and be friendly to the stranger.

How, from a dog's point of view, is he to know who are your friends and who are unwanted intruders? Some dogs undoubtedly seem to sense this by instinct. Most judge people by their scent, and we suspect that fear in humans produces a strong scent perceptible to dogs. Therefore I think we can conclude that an intruder facing a dog feels fear and sends out this scent, but I think people may only just not like dogs and also send out this scent although they are welcome on the premises. And so it seems sensible to me to train dogs to give warning barks at the approach of foe and friend and to stop doing so when told.

Burglars have been known to be great dog lovers and

have been welcomed by guard dogs, so I think it is difficult for a dog to know a burglar all by himself. Having trained your dog to bark, he should clearly understand his duty and beyond that we needn't go.

Special guard dogs must receive specialised training for their work, and that training is not for the ordinary owner to teach. It is a very personal and rigid training only to be undertaken by experts for experienced handlers to work the dogs, never for the ordinary householder, for a guard dog is potentially dangerous and ordinary people couldn't manage them, and don't live under suitable conditions to keep one.

The dog's mind should understand that his owner only needs a warning of approach of anyone, and not a bite. I am sure any beloved owner would get full protection from an adult dog if he had been trained to give warning from an early age.

If he shows no signs of being a natural guard don't let him have the run of the garden, teach him in the house by praise and encouragement if he shows any signs of barking whatsoever. If you have two dogs the older one will teach the young one, but two scatty dogs in a garden can be a double menace, and much more difficult to cure of going for strangers in a menacing way.

When dogs go for me I feel no fear and grab them and give them a good shaking. I have been bitten, but not very often and I certainly don't feel it until after I have carried out my job. The result is, the dog gets a wholesome respect for the human who shakes it and is wary of others, and very often one shaking makes it completely change its ideas about attacking. Unfortunately we can't ask the tradesmen to do likewise, so all I can suggest is that the owner must get expert help and advice if troubled with an overzealous guard dog.

Some dogs will never guard at all, their natures are so friendly that they love all the world; the only thing is to get another dog as well or have a private line to Scotland Yard.

Theft

Thieving is a natural instinct in all dogs. From the earliest days in the nest he has had to fight for his existence. In the days of the wild pack his ancestors hunted and stole from those other animals not clever enough to guard their prey. The instinct to steal is strong in the dog. The dog's mind is cunning in stealing and hiding for future use either food or some article he fancies.

Much of it in the domestic dog today is done purely out of boredom. I have never know a well-trained dog, whose day is fully mapped out for it, steal. But the busy house-wife, who owns a dog purely for the children to play with, often gets a thief as a result of lack of deep affection for anyone in particular by the dog, and from being bored with no work to do.

All dogs should have work to do, whether it be only tricks to learn from the children or obedience exercises or some real work like gun work, etc. Without this, their brains are wasted, their minds pretty empty and their cunning increases. Watch how a thief dog sleeps almost with one eye open to deceive its owner into thinking it is fast asleep when what it is really waiting for is the opportunity to slip into the chickens' yard and steal their food, or into the owner's kitchen to see 'what's cooking' and to take whatever has been carelessly left about. The obvious fear on the dog's part when caught makes us realise dogs do know the difference between right and wrong if caught in the act or even if heading for where the act is to take place. Obviously, to know they are doing wrong, they must at sometime or other have been scolded or punished for this selfsame act.

Dogs aren't born knowing what or what not to do, they only learn like children. Having once been punished, dogs remember, but like children they hope they won't be caught in the act. Dogs can be so conscience-stricken that I have seen an innocent one creep and crawl away in shame when another dog has committed a crime, and the innocent dog has been punished in error.

I always remember as small children we had a big and a little dog. The big one had her puppies in the barn and rushed out when a tramp came too near, bit him, and streaked back before the tramp knew which dog had bitten him; the tiny one just stood there and watched. The tramp swore black and blue it was the little dog that had done the deed and if I had not seen the other one do it the little one would have been punished.

Sometimes dogs steal for praiseworthy motives. Earlier in this book I mentioned Argus my Alsatian who with his mate made a nest for their family. When Andy, his mate, had her puppies down that burrow, Argus, never having stolen before ,went through a phase of thieving. One day I saw him steal some meat off the kitchen table and streak out to the orchard and drop it at the hole of the family and bark. I never scolded him for I knew in this case nature and the instinct to provide for his family was above all the training he had received.

I think, therefore, owners should try and find the reason for the theft before correcting the dog. Sometimes worms produce a terrible hunger in dogs and a depraved appetite. When cured of these the dog no longer steals. Only punish when you are sure you as owner have not neglected your dog.

13

The Mind of the Owner

Having, I hope, in the earlier twelve chapters of this book outlined the way a dog's mind works in a number of actions and incidents, I feel no book of this sort would be complete without a little probing into the minds of a cross section of owners.

No one in particular comes to my mind as I write, just a motley of dog owners and dog lovers I have met in the past thirty years of loving dogs. Some of them have thrilled me, some have shocked me. On meeting some I have been sorry for their dogs, with others I would almost like to change places with their dogs, or at least be re-incarnated as their dog.

The thing that has always struck me forcibly is how awful it must be to be a dog. You don't chose the home you live in, nor the owner. If you want to leave it, you run away or commit crimes for which you get punished. If you run away you are either taken back to the same unsavoury home or given away to one that may prove just as horrid or, if not claimed or found another home, your short life on this earth may be ended for you by the Police or a Welfare Society.

You can't argue with your owner except by refusing to carry out commands or, in worse cases, biting the person you disagree with. You can't speak, so a psychiatrist can't help you. The vet only examines you and gives an opinion as to your state of health. A trainer may or may not understand you and for brief moments give you supreme happiness or dejected hopelessness. Yet with all the troubles in the world you are always ready to give unbounding love and affection to those to whom you belong, if only they will understand you. You can read the mind of your owner and all with whom you come in contact, yet your simplest wants are often misunderstood by humans.

You are always interested in things like smells which human beings seem to totally disregard and, if a certain smell particularly interests you so that you don't even hear your owner calling, you will have a cross owner.

You often get left behind suddenly in a strange boarding kennel with people you may not know or like and a multitude of other dogs who are also bewildered by the action of their owners. You show how upset you were when they do eventually come and fetch you by an overpowering welcome, yet the same thing happens again and the owners seem to completely misunderstand your dread of being deserted. Weeks before they leave you, you have picked up by telepathy the unrest in the household as the time approaches for their departure, and you know you are to be left once more with strangers, with no assurance that you will ever see your owners again.

You are encouraged to defend your home, yet, if you defend it too well and bite that nasty-looking man in a black hat who swaggers up the drive, you are punished for biting and probably shut up somewhere. How were you to know which people needed biting and which people just needed frightening?

Yes, I am afraid the life of a dog is a hard one.

What I as a trainer cannot understand about owners' minds is what they really wish us trainers to do or, better still, how they expect us to carry out our work without apparently correcting a dog or its owner.

As far as I can make out, if you correct their children, you are almost hated, if you correct their dogs, they can hardly bear it. Do they honestly hope that, having spoilt the dog for anything up to five years, the trainer can alter all that without the willing co-operation of the owner? Many owners long to be co-operative, but their tender natures recoil at having a poor dumb animal treated firmly in spite of the fact the dog obviously prefers the trainer to themselves, and never shows the slightest sign of being frightened or hurt by the treatment it gets.

I suspect that what they would really like to see when they first arrive in school is the treatment of the dog to be exactly what they have always done at home but with an entirely different outcome, so that they needn't have to change their methods too drastically.

I believe one has to change completely most owners' ideas on what a dog likes to make certain the future for that dog and owners will be a happy one.

I have only in a very few cases found lack of co-operation from owners after two or three sessions of training when they appreciate that they knew little of a dog's mind.

I always hope that people bringing their dog for training will do so in the same frame of mind as they bring their children to the dentist or doctor, realising that to train a dog well and quickly needs 100% co-operation between dog owner and trainer. There may be a few bad trainers to whom training is only exploiting their ego or their business acumen but most trainers are real dog lovers to whom training is a calling.

Few owners realise that the training of dogs, if done conscientiously, is quite a dangerous occupation for the trainer and that, if they are bitten badly many times, it could lead to a lack of confidence in dogs which would be fatal for any trainer's work. Therefore the owner should want the dog to like the trainer and not be cross if it shows pleasure on being handled by the trainer. The owner should realise the association is only for a very short time and for the sole object of making owner and dog happy together. If this work can be done with the dog supremely happy in learning its lessons, it is nicer for the dog, although the owner naturally doesn't like sharing her dog's affection with a stranger.

Sometimes harsh things have to be done with dogs who are out of control. At these times the mind of the owner should try not to send out waves of horror, nor to think, 'I can't stand this, I shall take my dog home,' for soon the stormy scene will become a placid one and the dog taught for life that respect is necessary for true happiness.

Rushing from one training school to another only bewilders the dog, for every trainer has his own tried methods and is unlikely to be impressed or influenced by other ways that the owner may have been taught. Most trainers recognise that their pupils have been to another school so they shouldn't try and deny it, for dog trainers have long ago learnt that absolute honesty in dealing with dogs is essential; if the owner is a bit of a 'story-teller', her dog will not be the easiest to train.

The mind of the owner matters much more than the physical abilities, therefore never give up the thought of training your dog because you are not 100% fit. You can be helped to achieve the true companionship of a suitable dog. Unsuitable breeds should not if possible be bought by physically-handicapped or unfit owners. It is not fair to dog or owner.

Many trainers of dogs develop a marked telepathy with their pupils which also covers the owners' thoughts, so be careful what you are thinking in case the trainer can read your mind like a book.

And remember, if things get too bad, the owner can pay a visit to a psychiatrist, but I strongly recommend the dog stays at home. For the training of a dog by kind but firm methods is the best way to deal with any normal or problem dog. I believe the problems lie more with the owners than with the dogs. The day to day living conditions of many people are hardly suitable for a dog.

After all dogs were really meant to live natural lives whereby they probably ran at least twenty miles per day in pursuit of food. Their instincts were highly developed to gauge by scent alone the approach of danger, and their lives were fraught with risk of sudden death.

Now most of that is passed. The sniffing of a lamp post by a male dog not innoculated against Leptospirosis is far more likely to cause quick death than murder by another animal or human being. No longer can a dog wander off and fight to annex a wife for himself by sheer force of superior masculinity. He is expected to behave at all times like a gentleman and ignore the calls of nature. Do you wonder sometimes his mind gets a bit disturbed? He doesn't always fit into flat life in Kensington.

I think dogs on the whole are very accommodating creatures. They love human companionship, and endure hours of boredom in the hope that a walk or a game will come their way. They endure beauty treatment that in the past no self-respecting dog would have endured. They have to eat what is given to them instead of pouncing on the nearest sheep and gorging their tummies. And cats mustn't be chased.

In return for all this they get a warm comfortable home, vitaminised food of the right quality to ensure all their vital organs are sustained and nourished. They get as much exercise as the health and desire of their owner permit. They sometimes get unrestricted romps with interesting dogs and, if their owners are sensible, they learn their lessons like human children. Sometimes they get too little affection; often they get overwhelming affection which has exactly the opposite effect on a dog's mind to that the owner thinks it will have. Occasionally unfortunate dogs get only hatred, misunderstanding and despair for a bedfellow.

The mind of a dog is really very simple to understand. All it wants is someone to love and respect, a reasonable amount of fun, to be useful to its owner and to have a comfortable well-fed tummy. At certain times its mind runs almost exclusively on sex, then it is not easily controlled by the owner. On the whole the life of the dog and owner have to be in tune to get perfection out of the partnership. Both must respect each others likes and dislikes, and a deep understanding must exist between them.

There are many misfits in the canine and human world,

some that could never be put right. The putting of the dog to sleep, when it is often the owner's fault, has always seemed to me to be unfair but I doubt if in a civilised world it will ever be possible to have it the other way round.

14

Living with Mentally Unstable Dogs

Undoubtedly if we as a nation weren't such dog lovers people like me might be out of a job, for mentally unstable dogs abound these days. Some are born unstable, some are made unstable by their living conditions, but the result is the same: the dogs, instead of being a joy to their owners, are a worry, an expense, and often bring complete despair to the entire family, for few owners can believe the puppy that was so sweet at eight weeks old can be the vicious, nervous or cunning creature it is at eighteen months.

What I want to consider is that some people are determined to keep these dogs rather than admit defeat, or purely because their affection for them makes the idea of putting them down when so young quite out of the question. So now I want to discuss ways and means of living reasonably peacefully with mentally unstable dogs.

Let's take the dog first that shrieks in cars. Is his owner never to go for a car drive taking him with him? If training has proved completely ineffective, what is the answer? I think it is quite simple. First, the owner must study her own driving methods. Is she a bad driver, jamming on the brakes, accelerating suddenly, turning corners on one wheel, cursing other motorists who don't comply with her wishes? Well, that is the sort of motorist that makes dogs scream in cars. Once I was driven at night to the film studio with Juno my Great Dane. She had driven with me all her life, and had slept most of the miles we covered. This drive was a nightmare. The driver was nervous, she made me feel my end was near at least ten times in twenty-two miles. The dog picked up my nerves, braced her feet against the car door at every corner or red light, panted and showed obvious distress. Had she been a young dog she might have barked or whined in fear. The car was too small to allow me to turn round and comfort her, and the result was that we were wrecks when we arrived at our destination. This one drive with a bad driver had been enough to make my dog frightened, after which if I inadvertently braked suddenly she lost confidence and showed distress. It took me some weeks to get her confidence back by driving steadily.

Doesn't it make one realise how easily a highly strung dog can get in this state of nerves all the time if the driver of the car it is in is erratic? Therefore the first thing I would do, if I had a dog that jumps about or shrieks or barks in a car, is to re-assess my own standard of driving. Make an effort to drive with more thought for the nerves of the dog as well as for the safety of other road users.

In connection with this it often occurs that the husband of the driver, or the wife, nags perpetually whilst being driven, or automatically jams down an imaginary foot-brake. No one thinks either of these two things affect a dog, but they do. The mind of a dog is acutely tuned in to all brain reactions of its owners and a sense of anger or frustration on the part of a member of the family is quickly communicated to the dog.

Having examined your driving methods and found them

perfect, the next thing to do is to think how the dog can be kept quiet whilst you and the family enjoy themselves. Fighting him in the car will only bring forth anger from some member of the family unless they are all saints, and in any case any disturbance whilst driving is dangerous in these days of congested motoring, so I am not going to suggest that sort of cure. But what possible harm can there be in keeping tranquilisers for the dog? I don't recommend these as an alternative to training but, in this chapter, I am concluding that training has for some reason failed, probably due to the oversentimentality of the owner. But even an oversentimental owner couldn't object to giving a tranquilliser to a dog.

I can instantly hear people saying, 'But what happens if I only want to go on short journeys? The tranquilliser wouldn't have time to work and would last long after my journey is over.' Well, the answer to that is, why take the dog along with you? It is quite obviously no pleasure for you or the dog, so leave him at home where he is presumably happy. Then I hear the words, 'Oh, he shrieks at home if left by himself and I shall get summonsed by my neighbours if I do that.'

The only answer is to muzzle the dog if all training fails, or as a very last resort you can have his vocal cord nicked which in about five years scars over and the bark returns to normal but in the meantime dog and owner relax and one hopes in that time will have ceased to be a nuisance.

Contrary to what many people imagine I have known some dogs so treated and have always found them normal happy dogs with relaxed owners, and no one gets annoyed if the dog has to be left say in a flat alone, he is able to live his own excitable life without being a worry to his owners. The alternative was to put him to sleep. I think the dog would rather live.

But, once again, this isn't the end to the dog owner's troubles. The dog, left alone without being able to annoy the neighbours, may once again come out top dog by digging up the floor, chewing the mats, etc, so that it cannot be left alone with any degree of freedom, and the owner worries about what will happen when she is out. Once again the answer is to make somewhere either in house or garden dog proof. Either make a penfold netting run round an outhouse or kennel so that the dog can be free without being able to escape, or else do the same under the stairs or a kitchen cupboard or a wall-cupboard, confining the dog there for short spells when you are in the house so that he is happy and not afraid of being left. Then, when the day comes that you are going out for a couple of hours only, you can send him to his cubbyhole confident he will be happy there. Once you are sure your dog can do no harm, your whole state of mind will change. You will give to that dog assurance that he previously lacked, and the dog will soon lose all his faults.

That is what often happens when dogs are given away as unmanageable. A new home and owner does wonders. The dog gets less nervy if the new owner understands how to manage him, and it at once becomes a happy dog. There is no doubt about it, many owners and dogs are complete misfits and the dogs will never be happy or sane with them. If only the owners had to pass some sort of test before being paired up with a dog many unfortunate dogs would have better owners and many unlucky owners nicer dogs.

15

Dogs that hate Men or Women

This is the most peculiar form of instability in dogs. They seem to hate sex more than form and can be sweet and happy with a woman and nervous or vicious with the opposite sex. What form of neurosis causes this we don't know. What can an owner do to make a dog with this nature livable with? First, examine the owner's mind. Has she or he ever had a grudge against the opposite sex? Did an overpowering school mistress make the young boy or girl's life a misery? Does she boast that she is a women's woman or does she only get on with men? 'I never get on with women, my dear,' is almost certainly said by the type of owner that makes a dog hate women.

Alsatians are peculiar in this way and will hate men or women instinctively if thought transference comes from an owner with a similar dislike. So many women own Alsatians to show their superiority over their fellow men or women. They like big guard dogs, and the big guard dog thrives under this state of affairs and develops easily a dislike of the sex the owner wishes to dominate. Corgis do the same. I have particularly noted it in these two breeds, partly because they are highly intelligent breeds and telepathy is very marked and partly because the shepherding instinct is uppermost and they have a natural suspicion of strangers. Correct them firmly when young and one gets no further trouble. Revel in their suspicious natures and you will have dogs that hate men or women, usually women.

Now how do we live with such dogs? The world being what it is, we can't only mix with one sex. Even husbands or wives are a necessity and it is often against the one or the other that the particular hate is centred. I think the solution is either to send the dog to be boarded or trained by a person of the sex it hates, or else get friends of that sex to feed it or take it for walks. If it shows any signs of being vicious, muzzle it and send it out for a long walk with the person it dislikes. Greet joyously that person when he or she returns and praise the dog. Make the person pat the dog and praise it before saying goodbye and, if possible, give it its food.

I know there aren't many good friends who will do this for you but I think, if an advertisement was put in the local press, some dog lover would respond. It might even help to employ a 'dog sitter' of of the hated sex when you go out so that, when you were out, the only comfort the dog would get would be from the sex it dislikes. Only by being made to tolerate people will it respond. Obviously if the owner has been jilted and hates all men her dog will naturally pick up this feeling when the owner is talking to a man.

In nearly every case all these faults in dogs can be traced to some minor mental disturbance of the owner, though the owner may be unaware of it. I often ignore the dog, and ask the owner searching questions to probe why the dog is unbalanced. When I find out what is wrong with the owner the dog is automatically cured. Dogs mirror their owners' inner thoughts more than their looks, as some people say. A dog mirrors your soul, for you can't deceive animals even though you may think you can.

In some cases when dogs have been cruelly treated by men or women the resulting hate is purely and simply a natural fear. Then the only thing to do is train the dog firmly enough to make fear a thing of the past. Sympathy only makes things worse.

Take it to a club with the trainer of the hated sex. If the trainer is a real dog lover, get him or her to caress the dog and handle it as much as is possible in a training class. Once the dog has got confidence in a member of the hated sex you are half-way to curing it. The rest must come by constant mixing with people in crowded places where the dog hasn't time to distinguish men from women.

Undoubtedly this sex hatred is not a breeding fault as so many mentally unstable faults are, so it should be easily curable with expert help.

Never keep the dog away from the sex it hates, make it go amongst people all the time, especially if the dog hates children – another fault that comes from fear. Take the dog where children are coming out from school, playing fields, etc; daily doses of this will soon make familiarity breed contempt. Make sure first though that subconsciously the owner doesn't also hate children. If this is the case get someone who loves children to take the dog out and amongst them for you, someone who trusts the dog and won't automatically tighten the lead when children approach. If there is any risk of the dog biting a child, muzzle it. I always fail to understand why people imagine muzzles are cruel; they are of the greatest help in training a dog, for when the dog is muzzled the owner's mind can be carefree. Time and time again I have met people who quake in their shoes and protest when I muzzle a dog, yet in a few minutes the dog pays no attention to the muzzle and plays happily in it; most unstable dogs would be happier with a muzzle and a less worried owner.

16

Summing up

I cannot stress often enough that, if you wish to keep a dog that is not normal, you must face up to living a slightly restricted existence. Although *you* may love a subnormal dog, other people must not be inconvenienced by it. If your dog pounces on little dogs for no other reason than wishing to see them helpless on the ground, it is useless to explain to the owner of the little dog that your dog won't really hurt it, for even being pounced on is quite enough to terrify a little dog though it doesn't get bitten.

It is your duty to keep your dog on a lead and away from other people's dogs until such a time as it is cured of its bad habits. If it is unlikely ever to be cured, you must at all times see that it causes annoyance to no one you meet. I don't think there is anything that produces deeper rage in me than to have my well-behaved dog attacked by someone else's untrained and uncontrolled animal. Much as I love dogs I feel hatred at those times, more for the owner than the dog.

One person I know can only exercise his dog after midnight because it is so vicious that he cannot hold it on a lead when approaching another dog or person. The dog goes completely berserk. I wonder whether an animal of this nature should be kept. Is it a dog's life only to go for walks when most animals naturally are asleep? I think not, but the owner thinks it worthwhile and that's all there is to it.

This savage trait in dogs is terribly difficult to eradicate after the age of two. Up to that age there is a hope but, once a dog has got away with being savage for so long, the cure is usually only obtained by castration and rigorous training over a long period. To have allowed a dog to be savage for two years means the owner lacks responsibility in his or her duty towards her dog and the human race and is therefore unlikely to co-operate with either of the above cures.

Alas! The mind of a dog of this age is all-masterful. He has obtained supremacy over mankind and the canine race. As stags fight to the end, so will dogs and, if the dog is a big breed, the necessary strength needed to correct it is often absent in owner or trainer. It is for this reason alone that I think the dog should be put down. For there may come a day when the owner is ill and someone less efficient is left to cope with the dog. Then an accident may occur, perhaps even causing the death of another much-beloved dog.

People often mix up vices with unbalanced minds. The two things should never be confused. A dog that eats its own excreta or the droppings of farm animals hasn't an unbalanced mind. No training is likely to eradicate it completely, for this is a nutritional fault or an infection by parasites. Given sufficient minerals the dog will often become completely normal. If punished for these things the dog loses faith in his owner, he is only doing what nature urges him to do to find the necessary minerals his body needs. Without training, a dog will cease this filthy habit when the mineral balance of its body is corrected.

Instinct is perhaps the greatest factor controlling the mind of a dog. Self-preservation, the urge to reproduce, the wish to follow a strong leader, the use of the senses to read the secrets of nature are inborn in all dogs.

No one in his sense would punish a bitch for tearing the sofa to bits when she is immersed in that queer state the 'pseudo-pregnancy' and apparently about to give birth to phantom puppies. To her it is all very real, and even if you scold her for digging she will do it again when you are not there. If this does happen, the best thing to do is to keep her with you in these trying times. It only lasts about ten days and usually, if the bitch sleeps in your room, it doesn't seem to occur. But if left on her own, especially at night, she will make frantic efforts to make a nest with disastrous results to your furnishings. This is not a mental instability it is a hormone upset and will right itself. To be forewarned is to be forearmed. Either put her somewhere she can do no damage or keep her with you throughout her trying time.

Only the owners of unbalanced dogs can really know where the line can be drawn between a dog that is sane or mentally unsound. No one can make up the owner's mind as to what to do with the last kind. I, as a great dog lover, feel it is kinder to put them to sleep. There are so many nice dogs wanting homes without vice or instability who have no hope of life because they are unwanted. Surely, when all training and veterinary help has been exhausted and there is no hope of the dog living a reasonably normal existence, it is kinder to both to put the dog to sleep.

I believe that, if you understand how the mind of a dog works, you will not come up against many faults that cannot be cured or made liveable with under certain conditions. I do not believe a dog can be cured by a psychiatrist, but think some owners could be helped that way.

In the greater number of cases, a sensible attitude towards a dog's mind, not assuming it to be equal to that of a human being, is all that is necessary to insure that he will be throughout his life 'man's best friend', a joy to all and a nuisance to no one.